Sammel- und Bestimmungsbuch

für

Retro-Spiele

SEGA Master System I & II ©
SEGA Mega Drive / Genesis ©

© 2016 – Sammelland-Verlag Bad Vilbel
Michael Graf
Friedbergestr. 98
61118 Bad Vilbel
Tel: 0179/1473259
e-Mail: ep-verlagbadvilbel@web.de

Vorwort

Ein Bestimmungsbuch muss nicht teuer sein, um alle Bedürfnisse zu befriedigen. Der RETRO-Spiele Katalog beinhaltet die Spiele der beiden wichtigsten SEGA-Konsolen in PAL und NTSC.

SEGA Master System I & II (c)
SEGA Mega Drive / Genesis(c)

Was enthält der Katalog?
Mit diesem Buch wird gearbeitet! Alle Spiele sortiert nach Konsole und innerhalb der Kategorie nach dem Alphabet. Enthalten sind PAL und NTSC Spiele. Nicht enthalten sind asiatische oder lediglich in Südamerika erschienene Games.

Die Sammlung kann über simples ankreuzen verwaltet werden. Dies ermöglicht einen ständigen Überblick über den Zustand der einzelnen Spiele. Es ist kein Sammlerkatalog im Sinne der Wertbestimmung. Über jeder Seite ist diese Zeile zu sehen

PAL	NTSC	Name	Modul	Inlay	OVP

Man kann darunter ankreuzen, ob man das Modul, das Inlay und/oder die Verpackung in der Sammlung hat. Es sollte immer dabei sein, wenn man auf der Pirsch ist.

Die Rechte der hier aufgelisteten Namen liegen ausschließlich beim jeweiligen Lizenzinhaber. Der Sammelland-Verlag übernimmt keine Haftung für die Richtigkeit der in diesem Bestimmungsbuch gemachten Angaben.

SEGA Master System I & II ©

Technische Daten: 8 Bit Videospielkonsole
Auflösung: 256 x 240 Pixel
RAM: 64 KBit
CPU: 3,6 MZz
Speichermedium: Module und Karten
Verkaufte Einheiten: 13 Millionen

Zubehör:
- Light Gun
- SEGA Control Stick
- SEGA Commander Controller
- 3D Brille

PAL	NTSC	Name	Modul	Inlay	OVP
		Ace of Aces Sega 1991			
		Action Fighter Sega 1986			
		Addams Family, The Flying Edge 1993			
		Advanced Dungeons & Dragons: Heroes of the Lance U.S. Gold 1991			
		Aerial Assult Sega 1990			
		After Burner Sega 1990			
		Air Rescue Sega 1992			
		Aladdin, Disney´s Sega 1994			
		Alex Kidd: The Lost Stars Sega 1988			
		Alex Kidd in High-Tech World Sega 1989			
		Alex Kidd in Miracle World Sega 1986			
		Alex Kidd in Shinobi World Sega 1990			
		Alf Sega 1989			
		Alien 3 Arena Entertainmen 1992			
		Alien Storm Sega 1991			
		Alien Syndrome Sega 1987			

PAL	NTSC	Name	Modul	Inlay	OVP
		Altered Beast Sega 1988			
		Andre Agassi Tennis Tecmagik, Tec Toy 1993			
		Arcade Smash Hits Virgin 1992			
		Assault City Sega 1990			
		Asterix Sega 1991			
		Asterix and the great Rescue Sega, TecToy 1993			
		Asterix and the secret Mission Sega 1993			
		Astro Warrior Sega 1986			
		Astro Warrior /Pit Pot Sega 1987			
		Ayrton Senna´s Super Monaco GP II Sega 1992			
		Aztec Adventure – The golden Road to Paradise Sega 1987			
		Back to the Future II Image Works 1990			
		Back to the Future III Image Works 1991			
		Bank Panic Sega 1987			
		Basketball Nightmare Sega 1989			

PAL	NTSC	Name	Modul	Inlay	OVP
		Batman returns Sega 1992			
		Battle Out Run Sega 1989			
		Black Belt Sega 1986			
		Blade Eagle 3-D Sega 1988			
		Bomber Raid Activision Sega 1989			
		Bonanza Bros. Sega 1991			
		Bram Stoker's Dracula Sony 1993			
		Bubble Bobble Sega, Tec Toy, Taito 1988			
		Buggy Run Sega 1993			
		California Games Sega 1989			
		California Games 2 Sega 1993			
		Captain Silver Sega 1988			
		Casino Games Sega 1989			
		Castle of Illusion Starring Mickey Mouse Sega 1990			
		Champions of Europe Tecmagic 1992			

PAL	NTSC	Name	Modul	Inlay	OVP
		Championship Hockey U.S. Gold 1992			
		Chase H.Q. Sega 1991			
		Cheese Cat-Astrophe Starring Speedy Gonzales Sega 1995			
		Choplifter Sega 1986			
		Chuck Rock Virgin 1992			
		Chuck Rock II – Son of Chuck 1993			
		Cloud Master Sega 1989			
		Columns Sega 1990			
		Cool Spot Virgin 1993			
		Cosmic Spacehead Codemasters 1993			
		Cyber Shinobi, The Sega 1990			
		Cyborg Hunter Sega 1988			
		Daffy Duck in Hollywood Sega 1993			
		Danan: The Jungle Fighter Sega 1990			
		Dead Angle Sega 1989			

PAL	NTSC	Name	Modul	Inlay	OVP
		Deep Duck Trouble – Starring Donald Duck Sega 1993			
		Desert Speedtrap – Starring Road Runner & Wile E. Coyote Sega 1993			
		Desert Strike Domark 1992			
		Dick Tracy Sega 1990			
		Double Dragon Sega 1988			
		Double Hawk Sega 1990			
		Dr. Robotnik´s Mean Bean Machine Sega 1994			
		Dragon: The Bruce Lee Story Virgin 1995			
		Dragon Crystal Sega 1990			
		Dynamite Dux Sega 1989			
		Ecco the Dolphin Sega 1993			
		Enduro Racer Sega 1987			
		E-SWAT: Cyber Police Sega 1990			

PAL	NTSC	Name	Modul	Inlay	OVP
		F-16 Fighter Sega 1985			
		F1 Domark 1993			
		Fantastic Dizzy Codemasters 1993			
		Fantasy Zone Sega 1986			
		Fantasy Zone II – The Tears of Opa-Opa Sega 1987			
		Fantasy Zone: The Maze Opa Opa Sega 1987			
		Fire & Forget 2 Titus 1990			
		Flash, The Sega 1993			
		Flintstones, The Grandslam 1991			
		Forgotten Worlds Sega 1991			
		G-LOC: Air Battle Sega 1991			
		Gain Ground Sega 1990			
		Galaxy Force Activision, Sega 1989			
		Gangster Town Sega 1987			

MS 9

PAL	NTSC	Name	Modul	Inlay	OVP
		Gauntlet U.S. Gold 1990			
		Ghost House Sega 1986			
		Ghostbusters Sega 1987			
		Ghouls 'n Ghost Sega 1989			
		Global Defense Sega 1987			
		Global Gladiators Virgin 1993			
		Golden Axe Sega 1989			
		Golden Axe Warrior Sega 1991			
		Golfmania Sega 1990			
		Golvellius: Valley of Doom Sega 1988			
		GP Rider Sega 1993			
		Great Baseball –(Karte oder Modul) Sega 1987			
		Great Football Sega 1987			
		Great Golf Sega 1987			
		Great Ice Hockey Sega 1986			
		Great Soccer (Karte oder Modul) Sega 1985			

PAL	NTSC	Name	Modul	Inlay	OVP
		Great Volleyball Sega 1987			
		Hang-On (Karte oder Modul) Sega 1985			
		Hang-On / Astro Warrior Sega 1986			
		Hang-On / Safari Hunt Sega 1986			
		Home Alone Sega 1993			
		Impossible Mission U.S. Gold 1990			
		Incredible Crash Dummies, The Flying Edge 1993			
		Incredible Hulk, The U.S. Gold 1994			
		Indiana Jones and the Last Crusade U.S. Gold 1990			
		James Bond 007: The Duel Domark 1993			
		James Buster Douglas Knockout Boxing Sega 1990			
		James Pond 2: Codename RoboCod U.S. Gold 1993			

PAL	NTSC	Name	Modul	Inlay	OVP
		Joe Montana Football Sega 1991			
		Jungle Book, The Virgin 1993			
		Jurassic Park Sega 1993			
		Kenseiden Sega 1988			
		King's Quest I: Quest for the Crown Parker Brothers 1989			
		Klax Tengen 1991			
		Krusty's Fun House Acclaim 1992			
		Kung Fu Kid Sega 1987			
		Land of Illusion – Starring Mickey Mouse Sega 1992			
		Laser Ghost Sega 1991			
		Lemmings Sega 1992			
		Les Schtroumpfs Infogrames 1994			
		Les Schtroumpfs Autour du Monde Infogrames 1996			

PAL	NTSC	Name	Modul	Inlay	OVP
		Line of Fire Sega 1991			
		Lion King, The Virgin 1994			
		Lord of the Sword Sega 1988			
		Lucky Dime Caper – Starring Donald Duck Sega 1991			
		Marble Madness Virgin 1992			
		Marksman Shooting & Trap Shooting Sega 1986			
		Master Games 1 Sega 1993			
		Master of Darkness Sega 1992			
		Master of Combat Sega 1993			
		Maze Hunter 3-D Sega 1987			
		Mercs Sega 1991			
		Michael Jackson´s Moonwalker Sega 1990			
		Micro Machines Codemasters 1993			
		Miracle Warriors: Seal of the dark Lord Sega 1987			

MS 13

PAL	NTSC	Name	Modul	Inlay	OVP
		Missile Defense 3-D Sega 1987			
		Monopoly Sega 1987			
		Montezuma´s Revenge Parker Brothers 1989			
		Mortal Kombat Arena 1993			
		Mortal Kombat II Acclaim 1994			
		Ms. Pac-Man Tengen 1991			
		My Hero Sega 1986			
		New Zealand Story, The Tecmagik 1992			
		Ninja, The Sega 1986			
		Ninja Gaiden Sega 1990			
		Olympic Gold: Barcelona 92 Sega 1992			
		Operation Wolf Sega 1990			
		Ottifants, The Sega 1993			
		Out Run Sega 1987			

MS 14

PAL	NTSC	Name	Modul	Inlay	OVP
		Out Run 3-D Sega 1989			
		Out Run Europa U.S.Gold 1991			
		Pac-Mania Tengen 1991			
		Paperboy U.S. Gold 1990			
		Parlour Games Sega 1987			
		Penguin Land Sega 1987			
		PGA Tour Golf Tengen 1993			
		Phantasy Star Sega 1987			
		Pit-Fighter Domark 1991			
		Populous TecMagik 1991			
		Poseidon Wars 3-D Sega 1988			
		Power Strike Sega 1988			
		Power Strike II Sega 1993			
		Predator 2 Arena 1992			
		Prince of Persia Domark 1992			

PAL	NTSC	Name	Modul	Inlay	OVP
		Pro Wrestling Sega 1986			
		Psychic World Sega 1987			
		Psycho Fox Sega 1989			
		Putt & Putter Sega 1992			
		Quartet Sega 1987			
		R-Type Sega 1988			
		R.C. Grand Prix Seismic Software 1989			
		Rainbow Islands Sega 1993			
		Rambo – First Blood Sega 1986			
		Rambo III Sega 1988			
		Rampage Sega 1988			
		Rampart Tengen 1993			
		Rastan Sega 1988			
		Reggie Jackson Baseball Sega 1988			

PAL	NTSC	Name	Modul	Inlay	OVP
		Renegade Sega 1993			
		Rescue Mission Sega 1988			
		Road Rash U.S. Gold 1994			
		RoboCop 3 Flying Edge 1993			
		RoboCop vs The Terminator Virgin 1993			
		Rocky Sega 1987			
		Running Battle Sega 1991			
		Sagaia Sega 1992			
		Scramble Spirits Sega 1989			
		Sega Chess Sega 1991			
		Sega World Tournament Golf Sega 1993			
		Sensible Soccer Sony 1993			
		Shadow Dancer – The Secret of Shinobi Sega 1991			
		Shanghai Sega 1988			
		Shinobi Sega 1988			

PAL	NTSC	Name	Modul	Inlay	OVP
		Shooting Gallery Sega 1987			
		Simpsons, The - Bart vs. The Space Mutants Acclaim 1992			
		Simpsons, The – Bart vs. The World Acclaim 1993			
		Slap Shot Sega 1990			
		Snail Maze Sega 1986			
		Sonic Chaos Sega 1993			
		Sonic the Hedgehog Sega 1991			
		Sonic the Hedgehog 2 Sega 1992			
		Sonic the Hedgehog Spinball Sega 1993			
		Space Harrier Sega 1986			
		Space Harrier 3-D Sega 1988			
		Space Gun Taito Corporation 1992			
		Speedball Virgin 1991			
		Speedball 2 Virgin 1992			
		SpellCaster Sega 1988			

PAL	NTSC	Name	Modul	Inlay	OVP
		Spider-Man: Return of the Sinister Six Flying Edge 1992			
		Spider-Man, The Amazing vs The Kingpin Sega 1990			
		Sports Pad Football Sega 1987			
		Spy vs Spy (Karte oder Modul) Sega 1986			
		Star Wars U.S. Gold 1993			
		Streets of Rage Sega 1993			
		Streets of Rage 2 Sega 1993			
		Strider Sega 1991			
		Strider II Sega 1992			
		Submarine Attack Sega 1990			
		Summer Games Sega 1988			
		Super Kick Off U.S. Gold 1991			
		Super Monaco GP Sega 1990			
		Super Off Road U.S. Gold 1989			
		Super Smash T.V. Flying Edge 1992			

PAL	NTSC	Name	Modul	Inlay	OVP
		Super Space Invaders Domark 1991			
		Super Tennis Sega 1985			
		Supermann: The Man of Steel Sega / Virgin 1993			
		T2 – The Arcade Game Arena Entertainment 1993			
		Taz-Mania Sega 1992			
		Tecmo World Cup´93 Sega 1993			
		Teddy Boy Sego 1985			
		Tennis Ace Sega 1989			
		Terminator, The Virgin 1992			
		Terminator 2: Judgment Day Flying Edge 1993			
		Thunder Blade Sega 1988			
		Time Soldiers Sega 1989			
		Tom & Jerry: The Movie Sega 1992			
		TransBot Sega 1985			
		Trivial Pursuit: Genus Teque London Ltd. 1992			

MS 20

PAL	NTSC	Name	Modul	Inlay	OVP
		Ultima IV: Quest of the Avatar Sega 1990			
		Ultimate Soccer Sega 1993			
		Vigilante Sega 1988			
		Walter Payton Football Sega 1989			
		Wanted! Sega 1989			
		Where in the world is Camen Sandiego Parker Brothers 1989			
		Wimbledon Sega 1992			
		Wimbledon 2 Sega 1993			
		Winter Olympics U.S. Gold 1994			
		Wolfchild Virgin 1993			
		Wonder Boy Sega 1987			
		Wonder Boy in Monster Land Sega 1988			
		Wonder Boy III: The Dragons´s Trap Sega 1989			
		Wonder Boy in Monster World Sega 1993			

PAL	NTSC	Name	Modul	Inlay	OVP
		World Class Leader Board U.S. Gold 1991			
		World Cup USA 94 U.S. Gold 1994			
		World Cup Italia 90 Sega 1990			
		World Games Sega 1989			
		World Grand Prix Sega 1986			
		WWF WrestleMania: Steel Cage Challenge Flying Edge 1992			
		Xenon 2: Megablast Virgin 1991			
		Y´s: The Vanished Omens Sega 1988			
		Zaxxon 3-D Sega 1987			
		Zillion Sega 1987			
		Zillon II – The Tri Formation Sega 1987			
		Zool: Ninja of the Nth Dimension Gremlin Graphics 1993			

SEGA Mega Drive / Genesis ©

Technische Daten: 16 Bit Videospielkonsole
Auflösung: 320 x 240 Pixel
CPU: 7,6 MHz
Speichermedium: Module
Verkaufte Einheiten: 30 Millionen

Zubehör:
- Mega CD
- Master System Adapter
- Mega Power Stick
- Activator

PAL	NTSC	Name	Modul	Inlay	OVP
		3 Ninjas Kick Back Psygnosis 1994			
		6-Pak Sega 1995			
		688 Attack Sub Sega 1991			
		A Dinosaur´s Tale Hi Tech 1994			
		Aaahh! Real Monsters Viacom 1995			
		Action 52 Active Enterprises 1993			
		Addams Family, The Flying Edge 1994			
		Addams Family, The – Values Ocean 1995			
		Adventurs of Batman & Robin, The Sega 1995			
		Adventures of Mighty max, The Ocean 1994			
		Adventures of Rocky & Bullwinkle and Friends, The Absolute Entertainment 1994			
		Aero the Acro-Bat Sunsoft 1993			
		Aero the Acro-Bat 2 Sunsoft 1994			
		Aerobiz Koei 1992			
		Aerobiz Supersonic Koei 1993			

PAL	NTSC	Name	Modul	Inlay	OVP
		After Burner II Sega 1990			
		Air Buster Kaneko 1991			
		Air Diver Seismic 1990			
		Alex Kidd in the enchanted Castle Sega 1989			
		Alien 3 Arena 1993			
		Alien Soldier Sega 1995			
		Alien Storm Sega 1991			
		Alisia Dragoon Sega 1992			
		Altered Beast Seag 1988			
		American Gladiators GameTek 1992			
		Andre Agassi Tennis TecMagik 1992			
		Animaniacs Konami 1994			
		Another World Virgin 1991			
		Aquatic Games, The – Starring James Pond and the Aquabats EA 1992			
		Arcade Classics Sega 1996			

PAL	NTSC	Name	Modul	Inlay	OVP
		Arch Rivals: The Arcade Game Flying Edge 1992			
		Arcus Odyssey Renovation 1991			
		Ariel the little Mermaid Sega 1992			
		Arnold Palmer Tournament Golf Sega 1989			
		Arrow Flash Sega (PAL) – Renovation (NTSC) 1990			
		Art Alive! Sega 1991			
		Art of Fighting Sega 1994			
		Asterix and the great Rescue Sega 1993			
		Asterix and the Power of the Gods Sega 1995			
		Atomic Robo-Kid Treco 1990			
		Atomic Runner Sega 1992			
		ATP Tour Championship Tennis Sega 1994			
		Australian Rugby League EA 1994			
		Awesome Possum...Kicks Dr. Machino's Butt Tengen 1993			

PAL	NTSC	Name	Modul	Inlay	OVP
		B.O.B. EA 1993			
		Back to Future III Image Works 1991			
		Ball Jacks Namco 1993			
		Baltz 3D: The Battle of the Baltz Accolade 1994			
		Barbie: Super Model Hi Tech Expressions 1993			
		Barkley Shut Up and Jam! Sport Accolade 1994			
		Barkley Shut Up and Jam! 2 Sport Accolade 1995			
		Barney´s Hide and Seek Game Sega 1993			
		Bass Masters Classic Black Pearl 1994			
		Bass Masters Classic: Pro Edition Black Pearl 1995			
		Batman Sunsoft 1990			
		Batman Forever Acclaim 1995			
		Batman Returns Sega 1992			
		Batman – Revenge of the Joker Sunsoft 1992			
		Battle Master Arena 1990			

PAL	NTSC	Name	Modul	Inlay	OVP
		Battle Squadron EA 1990			
		Battletech: A Game of Armored Combat Extreme Entertainment 1994			
		Battletoads Sega 1992			
		Battletoads & Double Dragon Tradewest 1993			
		Beast Wrestler Renovation Products 1991			
		Beauty & The Beast: Belle´s Quest Sunsoft 1993			
		Beauty & The Beast: Roar of the Beast Sunsoft 1993			
		Beavis and Butthead Viacom 1994			
		Beggar Prince Super Fighter Team 2006			
		Berenstain Bears, The – Camping Adventures Sega 1993			
		Best of the Best: Championship Karate Electro Brain 1993			
		Beyond Oasis Sega 1994			
		Bible Adventures Wisdom Tree 1994			
		Bill Walsh College Football EA 1993			

PAL	NTSC	Name	Modul	Inlay	OVP
		Bill Walsh College Football 95 EA 1994			
		Bimini Run Nuvision 1990			
		Bio-Hazard Battle Sega 1992			
		Blades of Vengeance EA 1993			
		Blaster Master Sunsoft 1993			
		Blockout EA 1991			
		Blood Shot Domark 1994			
		Blue Almanac Super Fighter Team 2011			
		Bodycount Sega 1994			
		Bonanza Bros. Sega 1991			
		Boogerman: A Pick and Flick Adventure Interplay 1994			
		Boxing Legends of the Ring Electro Brain 1993			
		Bram Stoker's Dracula Sony 1993			
		Brett Hull Hockey 95 Sport Accolade 1994			
		Brian Lara Cricket Sportmaster 1994			

PAL	NTSC	Name	Modul	Inlay	OVP
		Brian Lara Cricket 96 Sportsmaster 1996			
		Brutal: Pawas of Fury GameTek 1994			
		Bubba´n´Stix Core Design 1994			
		Bubble and Squeak Sunsoft 1994			
		Bubsy in: Claws Encounters of the Furred Kind Accolade 1993			
		Bubsy II Accolade 1994			
		Buck Rogers: Countdown to Doomsday EA 1991			
		Budokan: The Martial Spirit EA 1990			
		Bugs Bunny in Double Trouble Sega 1996			
		Bulls versus Blazers and the NBA Playoffs EA 1993			
		Bulls vs. Lakers and the NBA Playoffs EASN 1991			
		Burning Force Namco 1990			
		Cadash Taito 1992			
		Caesars Palace Virgin 1993			

PAL	NTSC	Name	Modul	Inlay	OVP
		Cal Ripken Jr. Baseball Mindscape 1992			
		Caliber .50 Mentrix Software 1991			
		California Games Sega 1991			
		Cannon Fodder Virgin 1994			
		Captain America and the Avengers Data East 1992			
		Captain Planet Sega 1992			
		Castle of Illusion Starring Mickey Mouse Sega 1990			
		Castlevania: Bloodlines Konami 1994			
		Centurion: Defender of Rome EA 1991			
		Chakan: The Forever Man Sega 1992			
		Champions World Class Soccer Flying Edge 1994			
		Championship Bowling Mentrix 1993			
		Championship Pool Mindscape 1993			
		Championship Pro-Am Tradewest 1992			
		Chaos Engine, The MicroProse 1993			

PAL	NTSC	Name	Modul	Inlay	OVP
		Chase H.Q. II Taito 1992			
		Cheese Cat-Astrophe Starring Speedy Gonzales Sega 1995			
		Chester Cheetah: too Cool to Fool Kaneko 1993			
		Chester Cheetah: Wild Wild Quest Kaneko 1993			
		Chi Chi´s Pro Challenge Golf Virgin 1993			
		Chiki Chiki Boys Sega 1992			
		Chuck Rock Virgin 1991			
		Chuck Rock II: Son of Chuck Core Design / Virgin 1993			
		Clay-Fighter Interplay 1994			
		Cliffhanger Sony 1993			
		Clue Parker Brothers 1992			
		Coach K College Basketball EA 1995			
		College Football USA 96 EA 1995			
		College Football USA 97: The Road to New Orleans EA 1996			

PAL	NTSC	Name	Modul	Inlay	OVP
		College Football's National Championship Sega 1994			
		College Football's Nation Championship II Sega 1995			
		College Slam Acclaim 1996			
		Columns Sega 1990			
		Columns III Vic Tokai 1993			
		Combat Cars Accolade 1994			
		Comix Zone Sega 1995			
		Contra: Hard Corps Konami 1994			
		Cool Spot Virgin 1993			
		Cosmic Spacehead Codemasters 1993			
		Crack Down Sega 1990			
		CrossFire Kyugo Trading 1991			
		Crüe Ball EA 1992			
		Crusader of Centy Sega 1994			
		Crystal's Pony Tale Sega 1994			

PAL	NTSC	Name	Modul	Inlay	OVP
		Cutthroat Island Acclaim 1996			
		Cyberball Sega 1990			
		Cyber-Cop Virgin 1990			
		Cyborg Justice Sega 1993			
		Daffy Duck in Hollywood Sega 1994			
		Dark Castle EA 1991			
		Dashin´ Desperadoes Data East 1993			
		David Crane´s Amazing Tennis Absolute Entertainment 1992			
		David Robinson´s Supreme Court Sega 1992			
		Davis Cup World Tour Tengen 1993			
		Daze before Christmas Sunsoft 1994			
		Deadly Moves Kaneko 1992			
		Death and Return of Superman, The Acclaim 1994			
		Death Duel RazorSoft 1992			
		Decap Attack Sega 1990			

GEN 33

PAL	NTSC	Name	Modul	Inlay	OVP
		Demolition Man Acclaim 1995			
		Desert Demolition Starring Road Runner and Wile E. Coyote Sega 1994			
		Desert Strike: Return to the Gulf EA 1992			
		Devilish: The Next Possession Sage´s Creation 1992			
		Dick Tracy Sega 1991			
		Dick Vitale´s „Awesome Baby" College Hoops Time Warner 1994			
		Dino Dini´s Soccer Virgin 1994			
		Dino Land Renovation Products 1991			
		Dinosaurs for Hire Sega 1993			
		Disney´s Aladdin Sega 1993			
		Disney´s Pinoccio Disney Interactive 1996			
		Disney´s Bonkers Capcom 1994			
		DJ Boy Sega 1990			
		Donald in Mau Mallard Disney Interactive 1995			
		Double Clutch Sega 1993			

PAL	NTSC	Name	Modul	Inlay	OVP
		Double Dragon Ballistic 1992			
		Double Dragon 3: The Arcade Game Flying Edge 1992			
		Double Dragon V: The Shadow Falls Tradewest 1994			
		Double Dribble: The Playoff Edition Hyper Dunk Konami 1994			
		Dr. Robotnik´s Mean Bean Machine Sega 1992			
		Dragon Ball Z: Buyu Retsude Bandai 1994			
		Dragon´s Fury Tengen 1991			
		Dragon´s Revenge Tengen 1993			
		Dragon: The Bruce Lee Story Acclaim 1994			
		Duel, The: Test Drive II Ballistic 1992			
		Dune II: Battle for Arrakis Virgin 1993			
		Dungeons & Dragons: Warriors of the Eternal Sun Sega 1992			
		Dynamite Duke Sega 1990			
		Dynamite Headdy Sega 1994			

PAL	NTSC	Name	Modul	Inlay	OVP
		Earnest Evans Renovation Products 1992			
		Earth Defense Realtec 1995			
		Earthworm Jim Virgin 1994			
		Earthworm Jim 2 Virgin 1995			
		Ecco Jr. Sega 1995			
		Ecco the Dolpin Sega 1992			
		Ecco: The Tides of Time Sega 1994			
		El Viento Renovation Products 1991			
		Elemental Master Renovation Products 1990			
		ESPN Baseball Tonight Sony 1994			
		ESPN National Hockey Night Sony 1994			
		ESPN Speed World Sony 1994			
		ESPN Sundy Night NFL Sony 1994			
		ESWAT: City Under Siege Sega 1990			
		Eternal Champions Sega 1993			
		European Club Soccer Virgin 1992			

PAL	NTSC	Name	Modul	Inlay	OVP
		Evander Holyfield's Real Deal Boxing Sega 1992			
		Ex-Mutants Sega 1992			
		Exile Renovation Products 1991			
		Exo Squad Virgin 1995			
		Exodus Wisdom Tree 1993			
		F1 Domark 1993			
		F1 World Championship Edition Domark 1995			
		F-15 Strike Eagle II MicroProse 1993			
		F-22 Interceptor EA 1991			
		F-117 Night Storm EA 1993			
		Faery Tale Adventure, The EA 1991			
		Family Feud GameTek 1993			
		Fantasia Sega 1991			
		Fantastic Dizzy Codemasters 1993			
		Fatal Fury Sega 1993			

PAL	NTSC	Name	Modul	Inlay	OVP
		Fatal Fury 2 Sega 1994			
		Fatal Labyrinth Sega 1991			
		Fatal Rewind EA 1991			
		Ferrari Grand Prix Challenge Flying Edge 1992			
		FIFA 98: Road to World Cup EA 1997			
		FIFA Internation Soccer EA 1993			
		FIFA Soccer 95 EA 1994			
		FIFA Soccer 96 EA 1995			
		FIFA Soccer 97 EA 1996			
		Fighting Masters Treco 1991			
		Final Zone Renovation Products 1990			
		Fire Shark Sega 1990			
		Flashback: The Quest for Identity U.S. Gold 1993			
		Flicky Sega 1991			
		Flink Sony 1994			
		Flintstones, The Sega 1993			

PAL	NTSC	Name	Modul	Inlay	OVP
		Foreman for Real Acclaim 1995			
		Forgotten Worlds Sega 1989			
		Frank Thomas Big Hurt Baseball Acclaim 1995			
		Frog Feast Oldergames 2005			
		Frogger Majesco Sales 1998			
		Fun 'n Games Sony 1993			
		Funny World & Balloon Boy Realtec 1993			
		G-LOC: Air Battle Sega 1992			
		Gadget Twins, The GameTek 1992			
		Gaiares Renovation Products 1990			
		Gain Ground Sega 1991			
		Galaxy Force II Sega 1991			
		Garfield: Caught in the Act Sega 1995			
		Gargoyles Buena Vista 1995			
		Gauntlet IV Tengen 1993			

PAL	NTSC	Name	Modul	Inlay	OVP
		Gemfire Koei 1992			
		General Chaos EA 1993			
		Generations Lost Time Warner 1994			
		Genghis Khan II: Clan of the Gray Wolf Koei 1993			
		George Foreman´s KO Boxing Flying Edge 1992			
		Ghostbusters Sega 1990			
		Ghouls´n Ghosts Sega 1989			
		Global Gladiators Virgin 1992			
		Gley Lancer Sega 1992			
		Gods Accolade / Mindscape 1992			
		Golden Axe Sega 1989			
		Golden Axe II Sega 1991			
		Golden Axe III Sega 1993			
		Goofy´s Hysterical History Tour Absolute Entertainment 1994			
		Granada Renovation Products 1990			

PAL	NTSC	Name	Modul	Inlay	OVP
		Great Circus Mystery, The – Starring Mickey & Minnie Capcom 1994			
		Great Waldo Search, The THQ 1992			
		Greatest Heavyweights Sega 1993			
		Greendog: The Beached Surfer Dude Sega 1992			
		Grind Stormer Tengen 1994			
		Growl Taito 1991			
		Gunship U.S. Gold 1993			
		Gunstar Heroes Sega 1993			
		Gynoug Sega / DreamWorks 1991			
		Hard Drivin´ Tengen 1990			
		Hardball! Ballistic 1991			
		Hardball III Accolade 1993			
		Hardball 94 Sport Accolade 1994			
		Hardball 95 Sport Accolade 1995			
		Haunting starring Polterguy EA 1993			

PAL	NTSC	Name	Modul	Inlay	OVP
		Head-On Soccer / Fever Pitch Soccer U.S. Gold 1995			
		Heavy Nova Micronet 1991			
		Hellfire Sega 1990			
		Herzog Zwei Sega 1989			
		High Seas Havoc Codemasters 1993			
		Hit the Ice Taito 1992			
		Home Alone Sega 1992			
		Home Alone 2: Lost in New York Sega 1993			
		Hook Sony 1992			
		Humans, The GameTek 1992			
		Hurricanes U.S. Gold 1994			
		IMG International Tour Tennis EA 1994			
		Immortal, The EA 1991			
		Incredible Crash Dummies, The Flying Edge 1994			
		Incredible Hulk, The U.S. Gold 1994			

PAL	NTSC	Name	Modul	Inlay	OVP
		Indiana Jones and the Last Crusade U.S. Gold 1992			
		Insector X Sage´s Creation 1990			
		Instruments of Chaos starring Young Indiana Jones Sega 1994			
		International Rugby Domark 1993			
		International Sensible Soccer Limited Edition: World Champions Sony 1993			
		International Superstar Soccer Deluxe Konami 1996			
		Ishido: The Way of Stones Accolade 1990			
		Izzy´s Quest for the Olympic Rings U.S. Gold 1995			
		Jack Nicklaus Power Challenge Golf Accolade 1993			
		James „Buster" Douglas Knock Out Boxing Sega 1990			
		James Bond 007: The Duel Domark 1993			
		James Pond: Underwater Agent EA 1991			
		James Pond II: Codename: RoboCod EA 1991			
		James Pond 3: Operation Starfish EA 1993			
		Jammit Virgin 1994			

PAL	NTSC	Name	Modul	Inlay	OVP
		Jennifer Capriati Tennis Sega 1992			
		Jeopardy! GameTek 1992			
		Jeopardy! Deluxe Edition GameTek 1993			
		Jeopardy! Sports Edition GameTek 1993			
		Jerry Glanville´s Pigskin Footbrawl RazorSoft 1992			
		Jewel Master Sega 1991			
		Jimmy White´s „Whirlwind"Snooker Virgin 1994			
		Joe & Mac Takara 1994			
		Joe Montana Football Sega 1991			
		Joe Montana II: Sports Talk Football Sega 1991			
		John Madden American Football EA 1990			
		John Madden Football 92 EASN 1991			
		John Madden Football 93 EASN 1992			
		Jordan vs. Bird: One on One EA 1992			
		Joshua & the Battle of Jericho Wisdkom Tree 1994			
		Judge Dredd Acclaim 1995			

PAL	NTSC	Name	Modul	Inlay	OVP
		Junction Micronet 1990			
		Jungle Book, The Virgin 1994			
		Jungle Strike EA 1993			
		Jurassic Park Sega 1993			
		Jurassic Park: Rampage Edition Sega 1994			
		Justice League Task Force Acclaim 1995			
		Ka-Ge-Ki: Fists of Steel Sage's Creation 1991			
		Kawasaki SuperBike Challenge Time Warner 1994			
		Kick Off 3: European Challenge Vic Tokai 1994			
		Kid Chameleon Sega 1992			
		King of the Monssters Sega 1993			
		King of the Monsters 2 Takara 1994			
		King Salmon: The Big Catch Vic Tokai 1992			
		King's Bounty: The Conqueror's Quest EA 1991			
		Klax Tengen 1990			

PAL	NTSC	Name	Modul	Inlay	OVP
		König der Löwen, Der Virgin 1994			
		Krusty´s Super Fun House Flying Edge 1992			
		La Russa Baseball 95 EA 1994			
		Lakers versus Celtics and the NBA Playoffs EA 1990			
		Landstalker: The Treasures of King Nole Sega 1992			
		Last Action Hero Sony 1993			
		Last Battle Sega 1989			
		Der Rasenmähermann Time Warner 1994			
		Legend of Galahad, The EA 1992			
		Legend of Wukong Super Fighter Team 1996			
		Lemmings Psygnosis 1992			
		Lemmings 2 – The Tribes Psygnosis 1994			
		Lethal Enforcers Konami 1993			
		Lethal Enforcers II: Gunfighters Konami 1994			
		LHX Attack Chopper EA 1992			

PAL	NTSC	Name	Modul	Inlay	OVP
		Liberty of Death Koei 1994			
		Light Crusader Sega 1995			
		Lost Vikings, The Virgin 1993			
		Vergessene Welt: Jurassic Park Sega 1997			
		Lotus Turbo Challenge EA 1992			
		Lotus II – R.E.C.S. EA 1993			
		M-1 Abrams Battle Tank EA 1991			
		M.U.S.H.A. Seismic 1990			
		Madden NFL 94 EA 1994			
		Madden NFL 95 EA 1994			
		Madden NFL 96 EA 1995			
		Madden NFL 97 EA 1996			
		Madden NFL 98 EA 1997			
		Magic School Bus, The Space Exploration Game Sega 1995			

PAL	NTSC	Name	Modul	Inlay	OVP
		Man Overboard! S.S. Lucifer Codemasters 1994			
		Marble Madness EA 1991			
		Mario Andretti Racing EA 1994			
		Mario Lemieux Hockey Sega 1991			
		Markko´s Magic Football Marko Domark 1993			
		Marsupilami Sega 1995			
		Marvel Land – Talmit´s Adventure Namco 1991			
		Mary Shelley´s Frankenstein Sony 1994			
		Master of Monsters Renovation Products 1991			
		Marth Blaster – Episode 1 Davidson & Associates 1993			
		Mazin Saga – Mutant Fighter Sega 1993			
		McDonalds Treasure Land Adventure Sega 1993			
		Mega Bombermann Hudson Soft 1994			
		Mega-Lo-Mania Virgin 1992			
		Mega Man – The Wily Wars Capcom 1994			
		Mega SWIV Time Warner 1994			

PAL	NTSC	Name	Modul	Inlay	OVP
		Mega Turrican Data East 1995			
		Menacer 6-game Catridge Sega 1992			
		Mercs Capcom 1991			
		Michael Jackson´s Moonwalker Sega 1990			
		Mickey Mania: The Timeless Adventures of Mickey Mouse Sony 1994			
		Mickey´s Ultimate Challenge Hi Tech Expressions 1991			
		Micro Machines Codemasters 1993			
		Micro Machines 2 – Turbo Tournament Codemasters 1994			
		Micro Machines Military Codemasters 1996			
		Midnight Resistance Data East 1990			
		MiG-29 Fighter Pilot Domark 1993			
		Might and Magic II: Gates to another World EA 1991			
		Mighty Morphin Power Rangers Sega 1994			
		Mighty Morphin Power Rangers - The Movie Sega 1995			

PAL	NTSC	Name	Modul	Inlay	OVP
		Mike Ditka Power Football Accolade 1991			
		Minnesota Fats: Pool Legend Data East 1995			
		Miracle Piano, The – Teaching System Software Toolworks 1992			
		MLBPA Baseball EA 1994			
		MLBPA Sports Talk Baseball Sega 1995			
		Monopoly Parker Brothers 1992			
		Mortal Kombat Acclaim 1993			
		Mortal Kombat 2 Acclaim 1994			
		Mortal Kombat 3 Williams Entertainment 1995			
		Ms. Pac-Man Tengen 1991			
		Muhammad Ali Heavyweight Boxing Virgin 1992			
		Mutant Chronicles – Doom Troopers Playmates Interactive 1995			
		Mutant League Football EA 1993			
		Mutant League Hockey EA 1994			
		Mystic Defender Sega 1989			
		Mystical Fighter DreamWorks 1991			

PAL	NTSC	Name	Modul	Inlay	OVP
		NBA Action 94 Sega 1994			
		NBA Action 95 – Starring David Robinson Sega 1995			
		NBA All-Star Challenge Flying Edge 1992			
		NBA Hangtime Midway Home 1996			
		NBA Jam Arena Entertainment 1994			
		NBA Jam Tournament Edition Acclaim Entertainment 1994			
		NBA Live 95 EA 1994			
		NBA Live 96 EA 1995			
		NBA Live 97 EA 1996			
		NBA Live 98 EA 1997			
		NBA Showdown 94 EA 1994			
		NCAA Final Four Basketball Mindscape 1994			
		NCAA Football Mindscape 1994			
		Newmann/Haas Indy Car feat. Nigel Mansell Acclaim 1994			
		NFL 95 Sega 1994			

PAL	NTSC	Name	Modul	Inlay	OVP
		NFL Football 94 Starring Joe Montana Sega 1993			
		NFL Prime Time 98 Sega 1997			
		NFL Quarterback Club Acclaim 1994			
		NFL Quarterback Club 96 Acclaim 1995			
		NFL Sports Talk Football 93 Sega 1992			
		NHL 94 EA 1993			
		NHL 95 EA 1994			
		NHL 96 EA 1995			
		NHL 97 EA 1996			
		NHL 98 EA 1997			
		NHL All-Star Hockey 95 Sega 1995			
		NHL Hockey EA 1991			
		NHLPA Hockey 93 EA 1992			
		Nigel Mansell´s World Championship Racing Konami 1993			
		No Escape Psygnosis 1994			

PAL	NTSC	Name	Modul	Inlay	OVP
		Nobunaga´s Ambition Koei 1993			
		Normy´s Beach Babe-O-Rama EA 1994			
		Oh Mummy 1985 Alternativo 2012			
		Olympic Gold – Barcelona 92 U.S. Gold 1992			
		Olympic Summer Games – Atlanta 1996 Black Pearl Software 1996			
		Onslaught Ballistic 1991			
		Ooze, The Sega 1995			
		Operation Europe – Path to Victory Koei 1993			
		Ottifants, The Sega 1993			
		Outlander Mindscape 1992			
		OutRun Sega 1991			
		OutRun 2019 Sega 1993			
		OutRunners Data East 1994			
		P.T.O – Pacific Theater of Operations Koei 1992			

PAL	NTSC	Name	Modul	Inlay	OVP
		Pac-Attack Namco 1993			
		Pac-Man 2 – The New Adventures Namco Hometek 1994			
		Pac-Mania Tengen 1991			
		Pagemaster, The Fox Interactive 1994			
		Paperboy Tengen 1991			
		Paperboy 2 Tengen 1992			
		Pat Riley Basketball Sega 1990			
		Pepple Beach Golf Links Sega 1993			
		Pele II – World Tournament Soccer Accolade 1994			
		Pele! Accolade 1993			
		Pete Sampras Tennis Sportsmaster 1994			
		PGA European Tour EA 1994			
		PGA Tour 96 EA 1995			
		PGA Tour Golf EA 1991			
		PGA Tour Golf II EA 1992			
		PGA Tour Golf III EA 1994			

PAL	NTSC	Name	Modul	Inlay	OVP
		Phantasy Starr II Sega 1989			
		Phantasy Starr III – Generations of Doom Sega 1990			
		Phantasy Starr IV – The End of the Millenium Sega 1993			
		Phantom 2040 Viacom New Media 1995			
		Phelios Namco Hometek 1990			
		Pier Solar and the Great Architects WaterMelon 2010			
		Pink goes to Hollywood TecMagik 1993			
		Pirates of dark Water, The Sunsoft 1994			
		Pirates! Gold MicroProse 1993			
		Pit-Fighter Tengen 1991			
		Pitfall – The Mayan Adventure Activision 1995			
		Pocahontas Disney Interactive 1996			
		Populous EA 1990			
		Power Drive U.S. Gold 1994			
		Powermonger EA 1992			

PAL	NTSC	Name	Modul	Inlay	OVP
		Predator 2 Arena Entertainment 1992			
		Premier Manager Sega 1995			
		Premier Manager 97 Sega 1995			
		Primal Rage Time Warner 1995			
		Prime Time NFL Starring Deion Sanders Sega 1996			
		Prince of Persia Domark 1993			
		Pro Moves Soccer Asciiware 1994			
		Pro Quarterback Tradewest 1992			
		Pro Striker Final Stage Sega 1995			
		Psy-O-Blade Sigma Enterprises 1990			
		Psycho Pinball Codemasters 1994			
		Puggsy Psygnosis 1993			
		Punisher, The Capcom 1994			
		Quackshot starring Donald Duck Sega 1991			
		Quad Challenge Namco 1991			

PAL	NTSC	Name	Modul	Inlay	OVP
		R.B.I. Baseball 3 Tengen 1991			
		R.B.I. Baseball 4 Tengen 1992			
		R.B.I. Baseball 93 Tengen 1993			
		R.B.I. Baseball 94 Tengen 1994			
		Race Drivin´ Tengen 1993			
		Radical Rex Activision 1994			
		Raiden Trad Micronet 1991			
		Rambo III Sega 1989			
		Rampart Tengen 1991			
		Ranger X Sega 1993			
		Rastan Saga II Taito 1990			
		Red Zone Time Warner 1994			
		Ren & Stimpy – Stimpy´s Invention Sega 1993			
		Revenge of Shinobi, The Sega 1989			
		Revolution X Acclaim 1994			
		Richard Scarry´s Busytown Sega 1994			

PAL	NTSC	Name	Modul	Inlay	OVP
		Rings of Power EA 1991			
		Rise of the Robots Acclaim 1994			
		Risk Parker Brothers 1994			
		Risky Woods EA 1992			
		Ristar Sega 1995			
		Road Rash EA 1991			
		Road Rash 2 EA 1992			
		Road Rash 3 – Tour de Force EA 1995			
		RoadBlasters Tengen 1991			
		RoboCop 3 Flying Edge 1993			
		RoboCop Versus The Terminator Virgin 1993			
		Rock N´Roll Racing Interplay 1994			
		Rocket Knight Adventures Konami 1993			
		Roger Clemens MVP Baseball Flying Edge 1992			
		Rolling Thunder 2 Namco 1991			
		Rolling Thunder 3 Namco 1993			

PAL	NTSC	Name	Modul	Inlay	OVP
		Rolo to the Rescue EA 1992			
		Romance of the three Kingdoms II Koei 1991			
		Romance of the three Kingdoms III Dragon of Destiny Koei 1992			
		Rugby World Cup 95 EA 1994			
		Sagaia Taito 1990			
		Saint Sword Taito 1991			
		Sampras Tennis 96 Sportsmaster 1995			
		Samurai Showdown Takara 1994			
		Saturday Night Slam Masters Capcom 1994			
		Scooby-Doo Mystery Acclaim 1995			
		SeaQuest DSV Black Pearl 1994			
		Second Samura, The Vivid Image 1994			
		Sensible Soccer – European Champions Sony 1993			
		Sesame Street – Counting Cafe EA 1994			

PAL	NTSC	Name	Modul	Inlay	OVP
		Shadow Blasters Sigma Enterprises 1990			
		Shadow Dancer Sega 1990			
		Shadow of the Beast EA 1991			
		Shadow of the Beast 2 EA 1992			
		Shadowrun Sega 1994			
		Shanghai II: Dragon´s Eye Activision 1994			
		Shaq Fu EA 1994			
		Shining Force Sega 1993			
		Shining Force II Sega 1994			
		Shining in the Darkness Sega 1991			
		Shinobi III – Return of the Ninja Master Sega 1993			
		Shofe It! - The Warehouse Game DreamWorks 1990			
		Side Pocket Data East 1992			
		Simpsons, The – Bart vs the Space Mutants Acclaim 1992			
		Simpsons, the – Bart´s Nightmare Acclaim 1993			

PAL	NTSC	Name	Modul	Inlay	OVP
		Skeleton Krew Core Design 1995			
		Skeleton Krew Core Design 1995			
		Skitchin´ EA 1994			
		Slaughter Sport Razorsoft 1990			
		Smurfs, The Infogrames 1995			
		Smurfs, The – Tour of the World Infogrames 1996			
		Snake Rattle ´n´Roll Sega 1993			
		Snow Bros: Nick & Tom Tengen 1993			
		Sol-Deace Renovation Products 1992			
		Sonic 3D Blast Sega 1996			
		Sonic & Knuckles Sega 1994			
		Sonic the Hedgehog Sega 1991			
		Sonic the Hedgehog 2 Sega 1992			
		Sonic the Hedgehog 3 Sega 1994			
		Sonic the Hedgehog Spinball Sega 1993			
		Sonic Classics Sega 1997			

PAL	NTSC	Name	Modul	Inlay	OVP
		Sorcerer´s Kingdom Treco 1992			
		Space Harrier II Sega 1988			
		Space Invaders 91 Taito 1991			
		Sparkster Konami 1994			
		Speedball 2 Arena Entertainment 1993			
		Spider-Man – The Animated Series Acclaim 1993			
		Spider-Man vs. The Kingpin Sega 1991			
		Spider-Man and Venom – Maximum Carnage Acclaim 1994			
		Spider-Man and the X-Men – Arcade´s Revenge Flying Edge 1993			
		Spiritual Warfare Wisdom Tree 1994			
		Spirou Infogrames 1995			
		Splatterhouse 2 Namco 1992			
		Splatterhouse 3 Namco 1993			
		Spot Goes to Hollywood Virgin 1995			
		Star Control Accolade 1991			

PAL	NTSC	Name	Modul	Inlay	OVP
		Star Trek: Deep Space Nine – Crossroads of Time Playmates Interactive 1995			
		Star Trek: The next Generation – Echoes from the Past Sega 1994			
		Starflight EA 1991			
		Stargate Acclaim 1995			
		Steel Empire Acclaim 1994			
		Steel Talons Tengen 1992			
		Stormlord Razorsoft 1990			
		Street Fighter II – Special Champion Edition Capcom 1993			
		Street Racer Ubisoft 1995			
		Street Smart Treco 1991			
		Streets of Rage Sega 1991			
		Streets of Rage 2 Sega 1992			
		Streets of Rage 3 Sega 1994			
		Strider Hiryü Sega 1990			
		Strider II U.S. Gold 1992			

PAL	NTSC	Name	Modul	Inlay	OVP
		Striker Sega 1995			
		Sub-Terrania Sega 1993			
		Summer Challenge Accolade 1993			
		Sunset Riders Konami 1992			
		Super Baseball 2020 EA 1993			
		Super Battleship Mindscape 1993			
		Super Battletank – War in the Gulf Absolute Entertainment 1992			
		Super Fantasy Zone Sunsoft 1992			
		Super Hang-On Sega 1989			
		Super High Impact Acclaim 1992			
		Super Hydlide Seismic 1989			
		Super Kick Off U.S. Gold 1992			
		Super Monaco GP Sega 1990			
		Super Monaco GP II – Ayrton Senna´s Sega 1992			
		Super Off Road Ballistic 1992			
		Super Skidmarks Codemasters 1995			

PAL	NTSC	Name	Modul	Inlay	OVP
		Super Smash TV Acclaim Entertainment 1992			
		Super Street Fighter II Capcom 1994			
		Super Thunder Blade Sega 1988			
		Super Volleyball Sega 1991			
		Supermann – The Man of Steel Sunsoft 1992			
		Sword of Sodan EA 1990			
		Sword of Vermilion Sega 1989			
		Syd of Valis Renovation Products 1991			
		Sylvester and Tweety in Cagey Capers TecMagik 1994			
		Syndicate EA 1994			
		T2 – Terminator 2 – Judgement Day Flying Edge 1993			
		T2 – The Arcade Game Arena Entertainment 1992			
		TaleSpin Sega 1992			
		Target Earth DreamWorks 1990			
		Task Force Harrier EX Treco 1991			

PAL	NTSC	Name	Modul	Inlay	OVP
		Taz-Mania Sega 1992			
		Taz in Escape from Mars Sega 1994			
		Team USA Basketball EASN 1992			
		Technoclash EA 1993			
		Techno Cop RazorSoft 1990			
		Tecmo Super Baseball Tecmo 1994			
		Tecmo Super Bowl Tecmo 1993			
		Tecmo Super Bowl II – Special Edition Tecmo 1994			
		Tecmo Super Bowl III – Final Edition Tecmo 1995			
		Tecmo World Cup Atlus 1992			
		Teenage Mutant Hero Turtels – The Hyperstone Heist Konami 1992			
		Teenage Mutant Hero Turtels – Tournament Fighters Konami 1993			
		Terminator, The Virgin 1992			
		Theme Park EA 1995			
		Thomas the Tank Engine & Friends THQ 1993			

PAL	NTSC	Name	Modul	Inlay	OVP
		Thunder Force II Sega 1989			
		Thunder Force III Technosoft 1990			
		Thunder Force IV Sega 1992			
		ThunderFox Taito 1991			
		Time Dominator 1st Vic Tokai 1993			
		Time Killers Black Pearl 1996			
		Tinhead Spectrum HoloByte 1994			
		Tintin in Tibet Infogrames 1996			
		Tiny Toon Adventures – ACME All-Stars Konami 1994			
		TNN Bass Tournament of Champions American Softworks 1993			
		TNN Outdoors Bass Tournament 96 ASC Games 1996			
		Todd´s Adventures in Slime World Renovation Products 1992			
		ToeJam & Earl Sega 1991			
		ToeJam & Earl in Panic on Funktron Sega 1993			
		Toki: Going ape Spit Sega 1991			
		Tom & Jerry: Frantic Antics! Hi-Tech Expressions 1993			

PAL	NTSC	Name	Modul	Inlay	OVP
		Tommy Lasorda Baseball Sega 1989			
		Tony La Russa Baseball EA 1993			
		Top Gear 2 Vic Tokai 1994			
		Total Football Domark 1995			
		Toughman Contest EA 1995			
		Toxic Crusaders Sega 1992			
		Toy Story Disney Interactive 1996			
		Toys Absolute Entertainment 1993			
		Trampoline Terror! DreamWorks 1990			
		Traysia Renovation Products 1992			
		Triple Play 96 EA 1995			
		Triple Play – Gold Edition EA 1996			
		Trouble Shooter Vic Tokai 1991			
		Troy Aikman NFL Football Tradewest 1994			
		True Lies Acclaim 1995			
		Truxton Sega 1989			

PAL	NTSC	Name	Modul	Inlay	OVP
		Turbo Outrun Sega 1992			
		Turrican Accolade 1991			
		Twin Cobra – Desert Attack Helicopter Sega 1991			
		Twin Hawk Sega 1990			
		Two Crude Dudes Sega 1992			
		Two Tribes – Populous II Virgin 1993			
		Ultimate Mortal Kombat 3 Acclaim 1996			
		Ultimate Qix Taito 1991			
		Ultimate Soccer Sega 1993			
		Uncharted Waters Koei 1992			
		Uncharted Waters – New Horizons Koei 1994			
		Universal Soldier Ballistic 1992			
		Unnecessary Roughness 95 Sport Accolade 1994			
		Urban Strike EA 1994			

PAL	NTSC	Name	Modul	Inlay	OVP
		Valis Renovation Products 1991			
		Valis III Renovation Products 1991			
		Vapor Trail Renovation Products 1991			
		Vectorman Sega 1995			
		Vectorman 2 Sega 1996			
		Venom/Spider-Man – Separation Anxiety Acclaim 1995			
		Viewpoint Sammy 1994			
		Virtua Fighter 2 Sega 1996			
		Virtua Racing Sega 1994			
		Virtual Bart Acclaim 1994			
		Virtual Pinball EA 1993			
		VR Troopers Sega 1995			
		Wacky Worlds Creativity Studio Sega 1994			
		Wardner Mentrix Software 1991			
		Warlock Acclaim 1994			

PAL	NTSC	Name	Modul	Inlay	OVP
		WarpSpeed Accolade 1993			
		Warrior of Rome Micronet 1991			
		Warrior of Rome II Micronet 1992			
		Warsong Treco 1991			
		Wayne Gretzky and the NHLPA All-Stars Time Wanrer 1995			
		Wayne´s World THQ 1993			
		Weaponlord Namco 1995			
		Whac-a-Critter Realtec 1993			
		Wheel fo Fortune GameTek 1992			
		Where in the World ist Carmen Sandiego? EA 1992			
		Where in Time is Carmen Sandiego EA 1992			
		Whip Rush Renovation Products 1990			
		Williams Arcade´s Greatest Hits Midway 1996			
		Wimbledon Sega 1993			
		Winter Challenge Accolade 1992			

PAL	NTSC	Name	Modul	Inlay	OVP
		Winter Olympics – Lillehammer 94 U.S. Gold 1994			
		Wiz´n´Liz Psygnosis 1993			
		Wolfchild JVC 1992			
		Wolverine – Adamantium Rage Acclaim 1994			
		Wonder Boy III – Monster Lair Sega 1990			
		Wonder Boy in Monster World Sega 1991			
		World Championship Soccer Sega 1989			
		World Championship Soccer 2 Sega 1994			
		World Class Leaderboard Golf U.S. Gold 1992			
		World Cup USA 94 U.S. Gold 1992			
		World Heroes Sega 1994			
		World of Illusion Starring Mickey Mouse an Donald Duck Sega 1992			
		World Series Baseball Sega 1994			
		World Series Baseball 95 Sega 1995			
		World Series Baseball 96 Sega 1996			
		World Series Baseball 98 Sega 1997			

PAL	NTSC	Name	Modul	Inlay	OVP
		Worms Ocean 1995			
		Wrestleball Namco 1991			
		Wrestle War Sega 1991			
		WWF Raw Acclaim 1994			
		WWF Royal Rumble Flying Edge 1993			
		WWF Super WrestleMania Flying Edge 1992			
		WWF WrestleMania – The Arcade Game Acclaim 1995			
		X-Men Sega 1993			
		X-Men 2 – Clone Wars Sega 1995			
		X-Perts Deep Water 1996			
		Xenon 2 Megablast Virgin 1992			
		Yogi Bear – Cartoon Capers GameTek 1994			
		Ys III – Wanderers from Ys Renovation Products 1991			
		YuYu Hakusho – Gaiden Sega 1994			

PAL	NTSC	Name	Modul	Inlay	OVP
		Zany Golf EA 1990			
		Zero the Kamikaze Squirrel Sunsoft 1994			
		Zero Tolerance Accolade 1994			
		Zero Wing Sega 1991			
		Zombies ate my Neighbors Konami 1993			
		Zool EA 1993			
		Zoom! Sega 1989			
		Zoop Viacom New Media 1995			

Notizen

Herstellung und Verlag:
BoD - Books on Demand, Norderstedt
ISBN 978-3-7412-0489-0